Lidice

Lives

HEALING A NAZI MASSACRE

A TRAVEL PHOTO ART BOOK

LAINE CUNNINGHAM

Lidice Lives

Healing a Nazi Massacre

A Travel Photo Art Book

Published by Sun Dogs Creations
Changing the World One Book at a Time
Print ISBN: 9781946732965

Cover Design by Angel Leya

Copyright © 2019 Laine Cunningham

All rights reserved. No part of this book may be reproduced in any form or by any means, electronic, mechanical, digital, photocopying or recording, except for the inclusion in a review, without permission in writing from the publisher.

THE TRAVEL PHOTO ART SERIES

Bikes of Berlin
Necropolises of New Orleans I & II
Ruins of Rome I & II
Ancients of Assisi I & II
Panoramas of Portugal
Nuances of New York
Glimpses of Germany
Impressions of Italy
Altitudes of the Alps
Knights Through the Ages
Coast of California
Utopia of the Unicorn
Flourishes of France
Portraits of Paris
Tableaus of Tbilisi
Grandeur in the Republic of Georgia
Paragons of Prague
Hidden Prague
Lidice Lives
Along the Via Appia
The Pillars of the Bohemian Paradise
Terezín and Theresienstadt

Reinhard Heydrich, described by Hitler as "the man with the iron heart," was a German SS officer and a police official. He also chaired the Wannsee Conference, which laid out plans for the deportation and genocide of Jewish people. As Deputy Acting Reich-Protector of Bohemia and Moravia, he executed members of the Czech resistance.

WHAT ONCE WAS

DAYS BEFORE

HUNDREDS

BEYOND THE WALL

LOST

An assassination attempt was carried out against Heydrich on May 27, 1942. He died of his wounds a week later. Operation Anthropoid, the code name for the assassination, was carried out by Czechoslovak army soldiers who were in exile along with their government. The reprisal that followed targeted civilians.

ALSO

COMFORTLESS

SOLITARY

FRIENDSHIP

TOO MANY

Hitler wanted to slaughter 10,000 Czechs. But the area was an important industrial zone for the Reich. The deaths of so many forced laborers would reduce productivity. Instead, the tiny village of Lidice was targeted.

SHELTERING

RAZED

MARKERS

GHOSTLY

DEFENSELESS

Only days before the assault, the 340 citizens of the quiet village had no idea what was about to happen. Families rowed boats across the pond and laid out meals. Feed was strewn to the chickens and the spring crops were tended. Children studied their school assignments while adults chatted in the main square.

TINY TREASURES

DOVE

WELL

THE FLOWERS OF THE FIELD

Military trucks headed toward the village. Citizens woke to find tanks surrounding their tiny hamlet. Men and women were separated from each other. All men over the age of fifteen, 173 in all, were shot in front of a wall. The 203 women were deported to Ravensbrück concentration camp, while the 105 children were forced to work in a factory in Łódź before being gassed.

WASH AWAY

LOCKED

RESILIENT

The village was leveled. Buildings were torched before being torn down with explosives. Livestock and pets were killed. The bodies in the cemetery were exhumed, looted, and destroyed. The roads leading to and from the village as well as a stream were rerouted. Crops were planted atop the site to erase the last traces.

THE ROSE

SACRED

NEVER AGAIN

After the war, a handful of survivors returned. They rebuilt their beloved village a few miles away. Today their descendants live there, in the town called Lidice.

LIDICE LIVES

About the Author

Laine Cunningham leads readers around the world. *The Family Made of Dust* is set in the Australian Outback, while *Reparation* is a novel of the American Great Plains. Her travel memoir *Woman Alone* appeals to fans of *Wild* and *Eat Pray Love*.

Novels by Laine Cunningham

The Family Made of Dust

Beloved

Reparation

Other Books by Laine Cunningham

Woman Alone: A Six-Month Journey Through the Australian Outback

On the Wallaby Track

Seven Sisters: Spiritual Messages from Aboriginal Australia

Writing While Female or Black or Gay

The Zen of Travel
The Zen of Gardening
Zen in the Stable
The Zen of Chocolate
The Zen of Dogs

Bikes of Berlin
Necropolises of New Orleans I & II
Ruins of Rome I & II
Ancients of Assisi I & II
Panoramas of Portugal
Nuances of New York
Glimpses of Germany
Impressions of Italy
Altitudes of the Alps
Knights Through the Ages
Coast of California
Utopia of the Unicorn
Flourishes of France
Portraits of Paris
Tableaus of Tbilisi
Grandeur in the Republic of Georgia
Paragons of Prague
Hidden Prague
Lidice Lives
Along the Via Appia
The Pillars of the Bohemian Paradise
Terezín and Theresienstadt

The Wisdom of Puppies
The Wisdom of Babies
The Wisdom of Weddings

The Beautiful Book of Questions
The Beautiful Book for Dream Seekers
The Beautiful Book for Rebels
The Beautiful Book for Women
The Beautiful Book for Lovers

www.ingramcontent.com/pod-product-compliance
Lightning Source LLC
Chambersburg PA
CBHW041321110526
44591CB00021B/2860